The Score-Raising Vocabulary Builder for ACT and SAT Prep & Advanced SSAT and TOEFL Study

Level 1

Paul G Simpson IV

with

the Staff of Test Professors

Library of Congress Control Number: 2010942532

ISBN 978-0-9796786-4-6

For Faran

The Score-Raising Vocabulary Builder for ACT and SAT Prep & Advanced SSAT and TOEFL Study

Level 1

Table of Contents

LEVEL A VOCABULARY

TO EXPLAIN

Account For (verb)

The accountant could not <u>account for</u> the loss of his bank account.

Depict (verb)

She <u>depicted</u> the picture as a protest against the norms of the artist's society.

Other Common Forms: depiction (noun)

Illustrate (verb)

She <u>illustrated</u> her point by using colorful charts and lively video clips.

Other Common Forms: illustration (noun)

Point Out (verb)

The reporter <u>pointed out</u> the severity of the situation by comparing it to war.

Portray (verb)

While the foreign author <u>portrayed</u> the town as exciting, the locals disagreed.

Other Common Forms: portrayal (noun)

TO ARGUE FOR

Confirm (verb)

He could neither <u>confirm</u> nor deny whether he had been infirm in the hospital.

Other Common Forms: confirmation (noun)

Defend (verb)

He <u>defended</u> his plan to move to a deserted island by citing his need for solitude.

Other Common Forms: defense (noun)

Support (verb, noun)

Pippa <u>supported</u> the new law firmly, even going so far as to write several opinion pieces advocating its final passage.

Other Common Forms: supporting (adjective)

TO ARGUE AGAINST

Contradict (verb)

Angela <u>contradicted</u> her poor brother's vacation plans, noting that it currently costs several million dollars to take a trip to space.

Other Common Forms: contradiction (noun)

contradictory (adjective)

Counter (verb)

When Franklin could not <u>counter</u> his friend's very logical argument he was forced to remain silent.

Defy (verb)

Jae <u>defied</u> the social norms of his time by wearing his pants backwards and his shirts inside-out.

Other Common Forms: defiance (noun)

defiant(adjective)

Discredit (verb, noun)

The idea that no snowflake is the same as any other was <u>discredited</u> by scientists who captured two identical flakes.

Disprove (verb)

Although the student strongly contradicted the teacher's argument in the classroom, it was only after she was able to look up the relevant facts that she could definitively <u>disprove</u> it.

TO EMPHASIZE

Reinforce (verb)

Sophia made her point forcefully, <u>reinforcing</u> it by vigorously pounding her shoe on the table.

Other Common Forms: reinforcement (noun)

Stress (verb)

Sammy <u>stressed</u> how stressed he was in his new job by screaming loudly and ripping out several patches of his hair.

CONFUSED

Baffled (adjective)

The general was forced to retire after repeatedly being <u>baffled</u> in battle, unsure of where to direct his troops, or even how many troops were under his command.

Other Common Forms: bafflement (noun)

baffling (adjective)

Perplexed (adjective)

Paul <u>perplexed</u> the audience with a perfect puzzle: if a cat eats cheese, and no one sees it, is it full?

Other Common Forms: perplexity (noun)

perplexing (adjective)

Puzzled (adjective)

Rita found herself <u>puzzled</u> by the pain in her palm, until she realized how tightly she was gripping the airplane seat.

Other Common Forms: puzzlement (noun)

puzzling (adjective)

RAPID REVIEW #1

Find the synonym.

1) Perplexity
   (A) contradiction
   (B) reinforcement
   (C) puzzlement
   (D) illustration

2) Defy
   (A) portray
   (B) baffle
   (C) account for
   (D) counter

3) Stress
   (A) support
   (B) reinforce
   (C) depict
   (D) disprove

4) Point Out
   (A) depict
   (B) disprove
   (C) defend
   (D) puzzle

5) Confirmation

  (A) portrayal

  (B) perplexity

  (C) bafflement

  (D) defense

6) Counter

  (A) account for

  (B) defy

  (C) puzzle

  (D) portray

7) Reinforce

  (A) point out

  (B) contradict

  (C) disprove

  (D) stress

8) Depict

  (A) illustrate

  (B) support

  (C) baffle

  (D) counter

MOCKING

Ironic (adjective)

Sally was not insulted by her annoyed partner's remark because she understood it as a compliment instead of an <u>ironic</u> comment about her work ethic.

Other Common Forms: irony (noun)

Parody (noun, verb)

Though he had enjoyed some measure of success before, Peter Piper exploded in popularity after his <u>parody</u> of the president made millions laugh.

Other Common Forms: parodic (adjective)

Satirical (adjective)

Jonathan Swift's <u>satirical</u> "A Modest Proposal" was taken literally by many, causing them to recoil in horror at the idea of eating babies in order to alleviate famine.

Other Common Forms: satire (noun)

satirize (verb)

DOUBTFUL / QUESTIONING

Critical (adjective)

The judge earned a solid reputation as <u>critical</u> and fair, always willing to question the law and give an unbiased reputation.

Other Common Forms: criticism (noun)

critic (noun ⚥)

Hesitant (adjective)

Only when the team prepared to descend into the volcano did Victor, in a <u>hesitant</u> voice, finally ask the leader about the strength of the rubber bands tied around each member's waist.

Skeptical (adjective)

When her eight-year-old son detailed his plans to dig a hole to the center of the earth in order to mine gold, the mother gracefully hid her <u>skepticism</u> and handed him a shovel.

Other Common Forms: skepticism (noun)

skeptic (noun ⚥)

INDIFFERENT / LAZY

Dispirited (adjective)

Knowing that she had already lost the debate, Sheila put forth a most <u>dispirited</u> counter-argument that lacked energy and true conviction.

Dispassionate (adjective)

Having never tasted it before, Samuel was <u>dispassionate</u> about his co-worker's offer of free passion fruit, saying only "whatever".

Other Common Forms: dispassion (noun)

Uninterested (adjective)

Her uncle pretended to be <u>uninterested</u> in the score of the game during the family dinner, even as he checked it on his phone every two or three minutes.

PASSIONATE

Amorous (adjective)

His <u>amorous</u> glance across the river at his long-lost love was interrupted when he leaned too far and fell in.

Longing (noun, adjective)

Facing a stack of overdue bills on the table, Bridgette felt a great <u>longing</u> for the days when she had no financial responsibility.

Other Common Forms: to long (verb)

Yearning (noun, adjective)

Larry's <u>yearning</u> for learning drove him to read the entire Wikipedia site in all of its 272 different languages.

Other Common Forms: to yearn (verb)

TO PRAISE

Acclaim (noun, verb)

His longing for <u>acclaim</u> in the field of genetic engineering led Dr. Park to claim that he had successfully combined the DNA of a clam and a monkey for the first time.

Accolade (noun)

Winnie Suh's satirical take on the life of slugs, *It's a Slug's Life*, has received <u>accolades</u> and prizes around the world.

Applause (noun)

When the delighted audience members could <u>applaud</u> the spectacular movie no more due to hand and shoulder fatigue, they showed their appreciation with their feet.

Other Common Forms: applaud (verb)

Hail (verb)

The critics <u>hailed</u> the actor's role as the best dramatic performance of the century.

Laud (verb)

The tourists <u>lauded</u> Fort Lauderdale, giving it five-star reviews and highly recommending the city to others.

Other Common Forms: laudatory (adjective)

RAPID REVIEW #2

Find the synonym.

1) Acclaim
   (A) longing
   (B) criticism
   (C) irony
   (D) accolade

2) Dispassionate
   (A) laudatory
   (B) dispirited
   (C) amorous
   (D) skeptical

3) Yearn
   (A) satirize
   (B) applaud
   (C) long
   (D) laud

4) Skepticism
   (A) parody
   (B) criticism
   (C) applause
   (D) dispassion

5) Hail

   (A) yearn

   (B) parody

   (C) long

   (D) acclaim

6) Satirical

   (A) parodic

   (B) uninterested

   (C) laudatory

   (D) hesitant

7) Amorous

   (A) dispassionate

   (B) critical

   (C) dispirited

   (D) longing

8) Parody

   (A) acclaim

   (B) satire

   (C) skeptic

   (D) accolade

TO CRITICIZE / TO SCOLD

Admonish (verb)

The ad's director was <u>admonished</u> by critics who condemned the piece as not only tasteless but also nonsensical.

Other Common Forms: admonishment (noun)

Chastise (verb)

After hearing of his sister's decision to drop out of college to become a mule trainer, Chas <u>chastised</u> her for her choice.

Other Common Forms: chastisement (noun)

Rebuke (verb, noun)

After she turned down the substantial reward for finding the priceless violin, Michelle was <u>rebuked</u> by her friends, siblings, and second-cousins.

Reprimand (verb, noun)

Although not fired, Ronnie suffered severe <u>reprimands</u> from his bosses after it was discovered that he had stolen 2,718 Post-it notes from the supply office.

DISLIKE / HATE

Animosity (noun)

What appeared to be <u>animosity</u> between the two fierce rivals on the court was actually a manifestation of their desire to win.

Other Common Forms: animus (noun)

Antagonism (noun)

My aunt's <u>antagonism</u> towards ants only intensified after they carried away her carefully-prepared picnic lunch.

Other Common Forms: antagonize (verb)

Disinclination (noun)

Dad's <u>disinclination</u> for drying the dishes led to repeated arguments with mom, who was baffled by this reluctance.

Other Common Forms: disinclined (adjective)

TO FLATTER

Adulate (verb)

Addie's <u>adulation</u> of animators drove her to seek out and compliment them so excessively that they eventually felt it necessary to take out restraining orders against her.

> *Other Common Forms: adulation (noun)*
>
> *adulatory (adjective)*

Bootlick (verb)

Bobby earned a reputation as a <u>bootlicker</u> after he offered not just to buy the boss a cup of coffee but to pick, roast, and grind the coffee beans used to make the coffee.

> *Other Common Forms: bootlicker (noun ☥)*
>
> *bootlicking (adjective)*

Servile (adjective)

Though a servant, he was never <u>servile</u> and maintained his pride and dignity throughout his long service to the king.

> *Other Common Forms: servility (noun)*

TO INSULT

Scorn (verb, noun)

Upon its invention, the television was <u>scorned</u> by the media as a useless plaything that would have no impact upon society.

Other Common Forms: scornful (adjective)

Slight (verb, noun)

Since he was slight of build as a freshman, Michael Jordan did not make the basketball team, a <u>slight</u> that motivated him to work hard and succeed throughout his basketball career.

Spite (verb, noun)

Spitting has been used for untold centuries as an expression of the deepest <u>spite</u>.

Other Common Forms: spiteful (adjective)

Taunt (verb, noun)

The referees threw Terry out of the game after she <u>taunted</u> her opponents, first by shouting at their coach, and then by dancing on their team bench.

Other Common Forms: taunting (adjective)

SMART

Cunning (adjective, noun)

Leucochloridium paradoxum is a <u>cunning</u> parasite that forces its snail hosts to get eaten by birds, an outcome that completes the parasite's life cycle.

Genius (adjective, noun ⚓)

Jenny's financial <u>genius</u> became apparent when she generated millions of dollars in profit from generic juicers.

Shrewd (adjective)

In a <u>shrewd</u> move that would later make him the richest man in the United States, Bill Gates kept the copyright of his first operating system instead of selling it to IBM.

Other Common Forms: shrewdness (noun)

Wise (adjective)

It has been said that, while knowledge helps you make a living, only <u>wisdom</u> helps you make a life.

Other Common Forms: wisdom (noun)

RAPID REVIEW #3

Find the synonym.

1) Rebuke
   - (A) cunning
   - (B) taunt
   - (C) reprimand
   - (D) slight

2) Bootlick
   - (A) spite
   - (B) adulate
   - (C) antagonize
   - (D) admonish

3) Shrewd
   - (A) cunning
   - (B) servile
   - (C) disinclined
   - (D) scornful

4) Animosity
   - (A) genius
   - (B) rebuke
   - (C) adulation
   - (D) antagonism

5) Adulate

   (A) spite

   (B) bootlick

   (C) chastise

   (D) admonish

6) Chastisement

   (A) scorn

   (B) wisdom

   (C) animosity

   (D) rebuke

7) Slight

   (A) shrewdness

   (B) taunt

   (C) antagonism

   (D) servility

8) Spite

   (A) rebuke

   (B) cunning

   (C) bootlicker

   (D) slight

STUPID

Buffoon (noun ⚲)

Though portrayed as a <u>buffoon</u> by his contemporaries, Daniel K. Smith is now often viewed as a genius who predicted the rise of automated technology.

Other Common Forms: buffoonery (noun)

Dolt (noun ⚲)

Dan earned a reputation as the office <u>dolt</u> after he mislabeled all of the company's holiday cards and sent them to Cambodia.

Other Common Forms: doltishness (noun)

doltish (adjective)

Imbecilic (adjective)

The parents strained to reinforce the idea that they had not called their daughter <u>imbecilic</u> but rather her decision to steal the family car and crash it through the front of the local McDonald's.

Other Common Forms: imbecile (noun ⚲)

Obtuse (adjective)

While he was undoubtedly cunning in the classroom, Oliver failed his courses because he continued to be <u>obtuse</u> about completing his homework.

Other Common Forms: obtuseness (noun)

BRAVE

Bold (adjective)

Brian defended his quest to sail around the world in his bathtub as <u>bold</u>; skeptics, however, depicted it as imbecilic.

Other Common Forms: boldness (noun)

Gallant (adjective)

Medieval romances speak of <u>gallant</u> knights who perform deeds that normal men fear to even try.

Other Common Forms: gallantry (noun)

Resolute (adjective)

Ignoring detractors who predicted that they would never succeed, the Wright Brothers remained <u>resolute</u> in their determination to fly.

Other Common Forms: resoluteness (noun)

DIFFERENT / ODD

Abnormal (adjective)

After doctors discovered an <u>abnormal</u>, black-colored spot on her shoulder, Melanie underwent a test for melanoma.

Other Common Forms: abnormality (noun)

Deviant (adjective)

Those artists considered most <u>deviant</u> and strange by one generation almost always find themselves in the mainstream of the next generation.

Other Common Forms: deviance (noun)

deviate (verb)

Variant (noun, adjective)

The academic world shook with controversy when a <u>variant</u> text emerged in which it was not Mary, but Margaret, who had a little lamb.

WIDESPREAD / OBVIOUS

Blatant (adjective)

Barry voiced his displeasure with his friend in a <u>blatant</u> fashion, screaming at her so loudly that she finally hung up the phone.

Evident (adjective)

Tina's disinclination for liver was <u>evident</u> in her face, which puckered up and began to turn green.

Explicit (adjective)

By circling the prized bicycle in five different catalogs and leaving them next to his parents' bed, Eric made his Christmas wish quite <u>explicit</u>.

Other Common Forms: explicitness (noun)

SECRET / HARD TO UNDERSTAND

Covert (adjective)

The politician dismissed charges that her plans were <u>covert</u>, pointing out the fact that they had received in-depth coverage in all of the major newspapers.

Other Common Forms: covertness (noun)

Cryptic (adjective)

Finding her father's last words quite <u>cryptic</u>, Christine asked everyone she knew what her father could have meant by "Don't eat the cream cheese."

Stealthy (adjective)

In the wild, predators rely as much on luck as on <u>stealth</u>, the ability to keep their movements hidden from their prey.

Other Common Forms: stealth (noun)

LEVEL A REVIEW

Find the synonym.

1) Resolute
   (A) imbecilic
   (B) longing
   (C) gallant
   (D) puzzled

2) Obtuse
   (A) variant
   (B) blatant
   (C) servile
   (D) doltish

3) Cryptic
   (A) covert
   (B) supporting
   (C) adulatory
   (D) shrewd

4) Baffle
   (A) admonish
   (B) perplex
   (C) deviate
   (D) scorn

5) Deviant

   (A) evident

   (B) stealthy

   (C) defiant

   (D) abnormal

6) Servile

   (A) parodic

   (B) contradictory

   (C) bootlicking

   (D) shrewd

7) Accolade

   (A) explicitness

   (B) acclaim

   (C) chastisement

   (D) depiction

8) Gallant

   (A) blatant

   (B) spiteful

   (C) bold

   (D) amorous

9) Satirical

(A) explicit

(B) taunting

(C) baffling

(D) parodic

10) Depict

(A) portray

(B) rebuke

(C) counter

(D) defend

11) Dolt

(A) imbecile

(B) genius

(C) bootlicker

(D) skeptic

12) Rebuke

(A) obtuseness

(B) stealth

(C) applause

(D) reprimand

13) Discredit

   (A) slight

   (B) deviate

   (C) bafflement

   (D) contradict

14) Variant

   (A) resolute

   (B) abnormal

   (C) adulatory

   (D) laudatory

15) Covert

   (A) spiteful

   (B) ironic

   (C) dispirited

   (D) stealthy

16) Dispassionate

   (A) cunning

   (B) evident

   (C) uninterested

   (D) satirical

17) Yearn

    (A) laud

    (B) account for

    (C) chastise

    (D) long

18) Reinforce

    (A) illustrate

    (B) hail

    (C) satirize

    (D) stress

19) Perplexity

    (A) resoluteness

    (B) bafflement

    (C) covertness

    (D) doltishness

20) Acclaim

    (A) variant

    (B) animosity

    (C) accolade

    (D) parody

LEVEL B VOCABULARY

TO EXPLAIN

Clarify (verb)

Though Clarence tried to <u>clarify</u> the experiment to the class, his fellow students only left the class more perplexed.

Other Common Forms: clarification (noun)

Elucidate (verb)

After her son failed with a hands-on approach, Elsie <u>elucidated</u> the assembly instructions to him explicitly.

Other Common Forms: elucidation (noun)

Illuminate (verb)

That he is wearing a wetsuit and holding a penguin is <u>illuminated</u> by the fact that he is a trainer at the local aquarium.

Other Common Forms: illumination (noun)

Profile (verb, noun)

As part of his regular duties as a beat reporter, Craig had to consistently <u>profile</u> the latest changes in the law to his readers.

TO ARGUE FOR

Assert (verb)

He shrewdly <u>asserted</u> his right to call an attorney, citing the Supreme Court's decision in Miranda v. Arizona.

Other Common Forms: assertion (noun)

Bolster (verb)

Billy planned to <u>bolster</u> his case for a higher allowance with detailed charts and graphs that would clarify his current poverty.

Contend (verb)

Diane's <u>contention</u> that she was managing her diabetes by limiting her sugar intake was undercut by the chocolate on her lips and the jelly donut stains on her pants.

Other Common Forms: contention (noun)

Justify (verb)

While many have countered the need for war in society, just as many have <u>justified</u> it as a legitimate and moral struggle.

Other Common Forms: justification (noun)

TO ARGUE AGAINST

Dismiss (verb)

The senator <u>dismissed</u> his staff's suggestion not with words but with a quick disgusted wave of his hand.

Other Common Forms: dismissal (noun)

Dispel (verb)

The notion that Sir Hillary Saint was the richest man in the town was <u>dispelled</u> when it was revealed that he owed more than 20 million dollars to his creditors.

Dispute (verb, noun)

The parties did not <u>dispute</u> that the toxic chemicals needed to be cleaned up but only the best manner in which to do so.

TO EMPHASIZE

Accentuate (verb)

Because she believed that it boosted her popularity, Fiona <u>accentuated</u> her Irish accent whenever she could.

Other Common Forms: accentuation (noun)

Reiterate (verb)

Despite the fact that his mother <u>reiterated</u> the need for sun block on the beach, Dustin did not use any and ended up with sunburn.

Other Common Forms: reiteration (noun)

Underscore (verb)

The village's need for clean drinking water was <u>underscored</u> by the fact that 72% of its residents contracted typhoid fever.

CONFUSED

Befuddled (adjective)

Since it was the middle of July, Brianna was <u>befuddled</u> by the Christmas catalogs that started to appear in her mailbox.

Other Common Forms: befuddlement (noun)

befuddle (verb)

Nonplussed (adjective)

Kate found herself <u>nonplussed</u> when her bank balance, which she expected to be in the millions, turned out to be less than ten dollars.

Quizzical (adjective)

Hyein's reaction upon opening her refrigerator and discovering a pair of shoes could only be described as <u>quizzical</u>.

RAPID REVIEW #5

Find the synonym.

1) Dismiss

   (A) illuminate

   (B) reiterate

   (C) dispel

   (D) contend

2) Elucidate

   (A) accentuate

   (B) profile

   (C) bolster

   (D) dispute

3) Quizzical

   (A) dismissive

   (B) illuminating

   (C) befuddled

   (D) clarifying

4) Accentuate

   (A) nonplus

   (B) assert

   (C) underscore

   (D) dispel

5) Justification

   (A) accentuation

   (B) perplexity

   (C) contention

   (D) profile

6) Nonplus

   (A) reiterate

   (B) befuddle

   (C) dismiss

   (D) elucidate

7) Dispute

   (A) dispel

   (B) underscore

   (C) illuminate

   (D) assert

8) Clarify

   (A) accentuate

   (B) elucidate

   (C) bolster

   (D) contend

MOCKING

Jeering (adjective)

Jackie Robinson ignored the <u>jeering</u> and the insults heaped upon him from the stands in order to become a Hall-of-Fame baseball player.

Other Common Forms: jeer (noun, verb)

Scornful (adjective)

The judge did not just reject the lawyer's imbecilic argument; she dismissed it with outright <u>scorn</u>.

Other Common Forms: scorn (noun, verb)

Spoof (verb, noun)

Every week the comedic actors <u>spoof</u> prominent political figures and their recent actions.

DOUBTFUL / QUESTIONING

Cynical (adjective)

Though deeply <u>cynical</u> about the drug's therapeutic effects, Cyrus nonetheless tried it because he desperately wanted to relieve his pain.

Other Common Forms: cynic (noun ⚓)

Dubious (adjective)

Karen remained <u>dubious</u> of her friend's promise to tutor her in French, even after he called her to confirm the time.

Other Common Forms: dubiousness (noun)

INDIFFERENT / LAZY

Apathetic (adjective)

Socrates was so <u>apathetic</u> about his personal appearance that he rarely washed his clothes or bathed at all.

Other Common Forms: apathy (noun)

Jaded (adjective)

Even the most <u>jaded</u> of videogame players will be shocked by the quality and graphics of the new gaming system.

Lukewarm (adjective)

The singer imagined that the crowd yearned for his presence, so he was surprised by their <u>lukewarm</u> applause and scant attention.

Nonchalant (adjective)

Psychologists theorize that the things people say that they're most <u>nonchalant</u> about are actually the thing that they care about most deeply.

Other Common Forms: nonchalance (noun)

PASSIONATE

Ardent (adjective)

Even his most <u>ardent</u> followers could not support the movie star's decision to abandon his young children.

Zeal (noun)

Hanna hated raw food, so it was with something less than <u>zeal</u> that she looked down at the plate of sushi before her.

Other Common Forms: zealous (adjective)

Zest (noun)

Lisa admired the way her co-worker approached every task, no matter how small, with <u>zest</u> and cheer.

Other Common Forms: zestful (adjective)

TO PRAISE

Commendation (noun)

After rescuing four dogs, three cats, and twelve monkeys from the illegal shop, Aaron received a <u>commendation</u> and a medal from the ASPCA.

Other Common Forms: commend (verb)

Eulogy (noun)

Amanda delivered a beautiful <u>eulogy</u>, full of respect and praise for a man who had dedicated his life to the service of others.

Other Common Forms: eulogize (verb)

Exalt (verb)

As a favor to his former student, Mr. Andrews <u>exalted</u> her in the strongest possible terms to the college admissions committee.

Other Common Forms: exaltation (noun)

Extol (verb)

Around 3 AM, on virtually every TV channel, one can find people <u>extolling</u> the virtues of such products as pocket fishing poles, exercise machines, and super washcloths.

RAPID REVIEW #6

Find the synonym.

1) Commend

   (A) jeer

   (B) scorn

   (C) spoof

   (D) extol

2) Dubious

   (A) apathetic

   (B) cynical

   (C) account for

   (D) zealous

3) Zeal

   (A) zest

   (B) eulogy

   (C) scorn

   (D) commendation

4) Jeer

   (A) exalt

   (B) extol

   (C) scorn

   (D) spoof

5) Lukewarm

   (A) dubious

   (B) ardent

   (C) zestful

   (D) nonchalant

6) Apathetic

   (A) jaded

   (B) cynical

   (C) zealous

   (D) jeering

7) Ardent

   (A) nonchalant

   (B) scornful

   (C) zestful

   (D) lukewarm

8) Spoof

   (A) eulogize

   (B) jeer

   (C) commend

   (D) exalt

TO CRITICIZE / TO SCOLD

Castigate (verb)

Angie's friends <u>castigated</u> her for not signing up for the audition, particularly when she had so much more talent than the other contestants.

Other Common Forms: castigation (noun)

Censure (verb, noun)

The officer was officially <u>censured</u> by the department after it was discovered that he had accepted multiple bribes.

Decry (verb)

Parents often <u>decry</u> video game for the harm they cause, even though studies show that such games actually improve hand-eye coordination and focus.

Reproach (verb, noun)

The coach <u>reproached</u> his players for their apathy and general nonchalance towards the game, which had resulted in them losing the football game by 74 points.

Other Common Forms: reproachful (adjective)

DISLIKE / HATE

Abhor (verb)

Abby <u>abhorred</u> apples to the point that she gagged at the mere mention of them.

Other Common Forms: abhorrence (noun)

Deplore (verb)

The crew <u>deplored</u> the arrogant explorer, who treated them with nothing but scorn and spite.

Other Common Forms: deplorable (adjective)

Detest (verb)

So much did Ashley <u>detest</u> the test that she said she would rather shave off her eyebrows than ever take it again.

Rancor (noun)

While he disliked all insects, Chris reserved his deepest <u>rancor</u> for cockroaches, which he found vile and repulsive.

Other Common Forms: rancorous (adjective)

TO FLATTER

Cajole (verb)

Through excessive compliments and praise, Dale was able to cajole his girlfriend into buying him a new car.

Coax (verb)

The director coaxed the actress into the disastrous movie role by wearing that she was the only one who could play the part and that the world deserved her gifts.

> *Other Common Forms: coaxing (noun, adjective)*

Lackey (noun ⚔)

Larry was content not to be the boss but the boss' lackey, who kept his position only through constant sweet-talk.

Toady (noun ⚔)

Though he had worked hard to earn his position as vice-president, he was commonly portrayed as a toady who held his position based solely on his ability to suck up to the president.

TO INSULT

Defame (verb)

She won the congressional race not because of her positions but because of her success in <u>defaming</u> her opponent's character.

Other Common Forms: defamation (noun)

Derision (noun)

Though the media is often <u>derided</u> as greedy and untrustworthy, the vast majority of the public continues to rely upon it for their information.

Other Common Forms: deride (verb)

Disparage (verb)

Though often <u>disparaged</u> as garbage, popular TV shows provide a social cohesion that is not easily replaced.

Other Common Forms: disparagement (noun)

Malign (verb)

Though it was <u>maligned</u> for more than a century in the United States, the idea of a woman's right to vote eventually gained momentum and became law in 1920.

SMART

Ingenious (adjective)

Not surprisingly, it was a math genius who had the <u>ingenious</u> idea for the lever, which has made all modern construction possible.

Sagacious (adjective)

Her ardent fans contend that Jane Austen should not be read for her knowledge but for her <u>sagacity,</u> the wisdom that still applies to life and human behavior today.

> *Other Common Forms: sage (noun ⚥)*
>
> *sagacity (noun)*

Sage (noun ⚥)

Thomas Jefferson's deep learning and shrewd politics earned him the nickname "The <u>Sage</u> of Monticello".

> *Other Common Forms: sagacious (adjective)*

RAPID REVIEW #7

Find the synonym.

1) Cajole

   (A) censure

   (B) coax

   (C) detest

   (D) malign

2) Decry

   (A) defame

   (B) abhor

   (C) deplore

   (D) censure

3) Derision

   (A) reproach

   (B) sagacity

   (C) disparagement

   (D) rancor

4) Sagacious

   (A) ingenious

   (B) deplorable

   (C) rancorous

   (D) coaxing

5) Rancor

    (A) censure

    (B) abhorrence

    (C) derision

    (D) toady

6) Lackey

    (A) sage

    (B) defamer

    (C) toady

    (D) castigator

7) Reproach

    (A) abhorrence

    (B) censure

    (C) rancor

    (D) sagacity

8) Disparage

    (A) cajole

    (B) deride

    (C) decry

    (D) detest

STUPID

Dullard (noun �)

The shrewd businessman often assumed the role of a <u>dullard</u> during negotiations in order to gain the advantages that came when his adversaries underestimated him.

Dupe (verb, noun �)

The man told the police that he felt like a <u>dupe</u> after he lost half a million dollars in a real-estate investment scam.

Vacuous (adjective)

Though critics decried it as <u>vacuous</u> and empty of any redeeming qualities, the book continued to climb the best-seller lists.

Other Common Forms: vacuity (noun)

BRAVE

Dauntless (adjective)

While his friends stood aside and simply watched, Tom dauntlessly ran between the two combatants and broke up their fight.

Other Common Forms: dauntlessness (noun)

Undaunted (adjective)

As she turned to page 3 of "War and Peace", Tiffany remained undaunted by the fact that she still had another 1472 pages to go.

Valiant (adjective)

Shawn explained valor not as the absence of fear but rather the overcoming of that fear.

Other Common Forms: valor (noun)

DIFFERENT / ODD

Discrepancy (noun)

After Summer noticed a <u>discrepancy</u> between her answer and the answer in the textbook, she redid the question until the solutions matched.

> *Other Common Forms: discrepant (adjective)*

Disparate (adjective)

Interviews have determined that people become doctors for <u>disparate</u> reasons; some do it for the prestige and money, while others do it to help people.

> *Other Common Forms: disparity (noun)*

Heterogeneous (adjective)

The school's student population was commended for its <u>heterogeneity</u>, with students from more than 120 countries.

> *Other Common Forms: heterogeneity (noun)*

WIDESPREAD / OBVIOUS

Conspicuous (adjective)

Dressed in a full chicken suit, Lily's presence at the business meeting was nothing if not <u>conspicuous</u>.

Other Common Forms: conspicuousness (noun)

Flagrant (adjective)

Faran was thrown out of the game for a <u>flagrant</u> foul, a violation so obvious to the entire crowd that there was no doubt.

Overt (adjective)

Alberto proposed to his girlfriend not in a low-key, private manner but rather in an <u>overt</u> fashion, arranging for the question to be written in the sky.

Other Common Forms: overtness (noun)

SECRET / HARD TO UNDERSTAND

Esoteric (adjective)

The mathematician quit his profession when the problems he was working on became so <u>esoteric</u> that only a few people in the entire world could understand them.

Furtive (adjective)

Devin glanced <u>furtively</u> at the paper of the student next to him, hoping to get the answer without getting caught.

Other Common Forms: furtiveness (noun)

Incognito (adjective)

The fugitive, who was wanted for crimes in Germany, lived <u>incognito</u> in rural China as an English teacher.

LEVEL B REVIEW

Find the synonym.

1) Accentuate

    (A) dupe

    (B) malign

    (C) reiterate

    (D) defame

2) Dubious

    (A) overt

    (B) cynical

    (C) dauntless

    (D) quizzical

3) Elucidate

    (A) disparage

    (B) justify

    (C) profile

    (D) dispute

4) Disparate

    (A) ardent

    (B) furtive

    (C) heterogeneous

    (D) reproachful

5) Esoteric

   (A) apathetic

   (B) coaxing

   (C) incognito

   (D) conspicuous

6) Vacuity

   (A) dupe

   (B) valor

   (C) disparagement

   (D) befuddlement

7) Toady

   (A) sage

   (B) dullard

   (C) lackey

   (D) cynic

8) Deplore

   (A) malign

   (B) abhor

   (C) cajole

   (D) bolster

9) Flagrant

   (A) nonplussed

   (B) nonchalant

   (C) overt

   (D) discrepant

10) Heterogeneous

   (A) furtive

   (B) ingenious

   (C) jeering

   (D) disparate

11) Coax

   (A) castigate

   (B) cajole

   (C) extol

   (D) dispel

12) Eulogy

   (A) defamation

   (B) justification

   (C) exaltation

   (D) derision

13) Reiterate

  (A) censure

  (B) detest

  (C) underscore

  (D) dismiss

14) Furtive

  (A) vacuous

  (B) lukewarm

  (C) sagacious

  (D) esoteric

15) Dauntless

  (A) heterogeneous

  (B) valiant

  (C) deplorable

  (D) quizzical

16) Castigate

  (A) deride

  (B) commend

  (C) reproach

  (D) contend

17) Clarification

    (A) nonchalance

    (B) rancor

    (C) conspicuousness

    (D) elucidation

18) Discrepancy

    (A) malign

    (B) disparity

    (C) spoof

    (D) exalt

19) Jaded

    (A) dauntlessness

    (B) apathetic

    (C) censure

    (D) accentuation

20) Nonplussed

    (A) esoteric

    (B) vacuous

    (C) quizzical

    (D) sagacious

LEVEL C VOCABULARY

TO EXPLAIN

Delineate (verb)

Linus <u>delineated</u> once more to his art students how to draw a proper line.

Other Common Forms: delineation (noun)

Demystify (verb)

The detective <u>demystified</u> the mystery to his colleague, explaining exactly what happened and when it happened.

Other Common Forms: demystification (noun)

Explicate (verb)

Gordon explained his theories to his friends, over and over again, until he felt that they were fully <u>explicated</u>.

Other Common Forms: explication (noun)

TO ARGUE FOR

Advocate (verb, noun ⚓)

Elizabeth was an <u>advocate</u> for the rescue of abandoned dogs, raising funds and managing a rescue operation.

Corroborate (verb)

Following the first witness on the stand, Jane <u>corroborated</u> his version of events completely and thoroughly.

Other Common Forms: corroboration (noun)

Substantiate (verb)

The mock-trial team <u>substantiated</u> its claims with scientific studies and expert testimony.

Other Common Forms: substantiation (noun)

Vindicate (verb)

The events of March 10, 1876 <u>vindicated</u> Bell's belief that the "multiple harmonic telegraph," or telephone, was possible.

Other Common Forms: vindication (noun)

TO ARGUE AGAINST

Debunk (verb)

Mary's belief in Santa Claus was <u>debunked</u> one fateful night when she saw twelve santas on the corner waiting for the bus.

Invalidate (verb)

The bank promptly <u>invalidated</u> Moe's ATM card after he failed to enter the correct password 247 times in a row.

Rebuff (verb, noun)

When he returned home after three days, Andrew's mom <u>rebuffed</u> his excuse that he had needed to go and buy hot dogs.

Rebut (verb)

Though she wanted to disprove her father's contention that she never did dishes, Monika could not <u>rebut</u> the fact that she had not picked up a sponge in over 5 years.

> *Other Common Forms: rebuttal (noun)*

Refute (verb)

Try as he might, Rufus could never <u>refute</u> the fact that gravity exists.

> *Other Common Forms: refutation (noun)*

TO EMPHASIZE

Highlight (verb)

The speaker <u>highlighted</u> his nonchalance about the presentation by yawning frequently and answering his cell phone several times.

Iterate (verb)

When the waitress failed to heed him, Nick was forced to keep <u>iterating</u> his request for more ketchup.

Other Common Forms: iteration (noun)

Punctuate (verb)

Nick <u>punctuated</u> his speech by shouting the words he felt were most important to communicate.

Other Common Forms: punctuation (noun)

CONFUSED

Confounded (adjective)

Though he successfully completed the first 30 questions, Patrick was truly confounded by the final problem, and finally gave up.

Other Common Forms: confounding (adjective)

Dumbfounded (adjective)

As she reached the edge of the sidewalk and looked up, Julia stopped dead in her tracks, dumbfounded by the sight of a parrot riding a bicycle backwards.

Other Common Forms: dumbfounding (adjective)

Vexed (adjective)

Since 1849 Polignac's conjecture has vexed mathematicians, who still cannot prove it.

Other Common Forms: vexing (adjective)

RAPID REVIEW #9

Find the synonym.

1) Punctuate

    (A) rebut

    (B) highlight

    (C) explicate

    (D) substantiate

2) Rebuff

    (A) iterate

    (B) invalidate

    (C) delineate

    (D) corroborate

3) Explication

    (A) rebuff

    (B) iteration

    (C) vindication

    (D) demystification

4) Dumbfounded

    (A) vindicating

    (B) confounded

    (C) refuting

    (D) substantiating

5) Refute

    (A) highlight

    (B) vindicate

    (C) debunk

    (D) delineate

6) Iterate

    (A) invalidate

    (B) punctuate

    (C) explicate

    (D) substantiate

7) Advocate

    (A) corroborate

    (B) refute

    (C) delineate

    (D) rebut

8) Debunk

    (A) confound

    (B) vex

    (C) rebuff

    (D) demystify

MOCKING

Derisive (adjective)

Michelle took offense not at failing to get hired for the job but for the <u>derisive</u> manner in which the interviewer informed her.

Other Common Forms: deride (verb)

Lampoon (verb, noun)

It has become tradition that the president <u>lampoon</u> himself and his administration once a year at the National Correspondents Dinner.

Scoff [at] (verb)

The arrogant leader <u>scoffed at</u> the idea that she could learn anything from her opponents.

Other Common Forms: scoffing (noun, adjective)

DOUBTFUL / QUESTIONING

Dubitable (adjective)

It was more than <u>dubitable</u> whether the rookie was as talented on the field as he thought he was.

Equivocal

The results of the test were open to <u>equivocation,</u> so the doctor strongly suggested that Tina take the TB test again.

> *Other Common Forms: equivocation (noun)*
>
> *equivocate (verb)*

Incredulous (adjective)

The announcement that cancer can be cured by tomatoes provoked an <u>incredulous</u> reaction from the scientific community, particularly since the study was funded entirely by the National Tomato Board.

> *Other Common Forms: incredulity (noun)*

INDIFFERENT / LAZY

Lackadaisical (adjective)

After he failed to prepare and often simply walked out of the classroom during class time, Alex was called to the principal's office to discuss his <u>lackadaisical</u> effort.

Languid (adjective)

After running two marathons that day, Alice was too <u>languid</u> to even shower and simply collapsed into bed.

Other Common Forms: languidness (noun)

Listless (adjective)

The sloth has a reputation as a <u>listless</u> animal because it sleeps 15 hours a day and its top speed is only 15 feet per minute.

Other Common Forms: listlessness (noun)

PASSIONATE

Avid (adjective)

Haleigh is an <u>avid</u> horse-racing fan, who spends every free minute watching or attending races.

Other Common Forms: avidness (noun)

Élan (noun)

Isaac always approached his work with great <u>élan</u>, a spirit that not only helped him to succeed but that also inspired others.

Fervidness (noun)

It was with deep <u>fervidness</u> that he knelt down and asked the heavens to win the 400 million dollar lottery jackpot.

Other Common Forms: fervid (adjective)

Fervor (noun)

Though the Civil War ended more than 150 years ago, it still provokes <u>fervor</u> among some citizens.

TO PRAISE

Approbation (noun)

So used to <u>approbation</u> was James that his parents' harsh castigation left him incredulous and speechless.

Kudos (noun)

Kiran received <u>kudos</u> from her teammates after she ended the game with a walk-off home run.

Panegyrize (verb)

After his death in 1963, John F. Kennedy was <u>panegyrized</u> formally by governments and reporters around the world.

Other Common Forms: panegyric (noun)

Plaudit (noun)

Upon their successful mission to the moon, the Apollo 11 astronauts received <u>plaudits</u> and fame.

Tout (verb)

The commercial <u>touted</u> the Ab-Chomper 24000 as the fastest and easiest way to work out one's stomach muscles.

RAPID REVIEW #10

Find the synonym.

1) Equivocal

    (A) avid

    (B) listless

    (C) dubitable

    (D) scoffing

2) Fervor

    (A) plaudit

    (B) élan

    (C) languidness

    (D) lampoon

3) Incredulity

    (A) plaudit

    (B) kudos

    (C) listlessness

    (D) equivocal

4) Scoff

    (A) tout

    (B) lampoon

    (C) deride

    (D) equivocate

5) Panegyric

   (A) languidness

   (B) approbation

   (C) élan

   (D) fervor

6) Languid

   (A) fervid

   (B) lackadaisical

   (C) dubitable

   (D) scoffing

7) Lampoon

   (A) panegyrize

   (B) equivocate

   (C) tout

   (D) deride

8) Kudos

   (A) avidness

   (B) listlessness

   (C) plaudit

   (D) incredulity

TO CRITICIZE / TO SCOLD

Berate (verb)

Jelani's father never <u>berates</u> him for failure but only for lack of effort and a lackadaisical attitude.

Excoriate (verb)

Upon hearing of the company's plans to dip baby turtles in oil and use them as lamps, environmentalists <u>excoriated</u> the company until it was forced to stop the project.

Other Common Forms: excoriation (noun)

Lambaste (verb)

Opposition party members <u>lambasted</u> Senator Lamb after it was discovered that she had accepted money and free vacations in exchange for her votes.

Reprove (verb)

Professor Red <u>reproved</u> his colleagues after they could not reproduce their results in the laboratory and, thus, left his theory unproven.

Upbraid (verb)

While she knew that her friend would be angry about the broken computer, Paula did not expect him to <u>upbraid</u> her for so long.

DISLIKE / HATE

Abominate (verb)

Though Abbott <u>abominated</u> peas with all of his being, he ate them at his grandmother's house in order to be polite.

Other Common Forms: abomination (noun)

Antipathy (noun)

Rather than sympathy for their needs, Addam held only the greatest <u>antipathy</u> towards the deer that repeatedly destroyed his prized garden.

Aversion (noun)

Albert's <u>aversion</u> to the new version of the game was most tellingly expressed when he stomped on it and then threw it in the trash.

Loathe (verb)

My aunt used to tell me: "Lots of <u>loathing</u> leaves you lonely, while lots of love leaves you laughing."

Other Common Forms: loathing (noun)

TO FLATTER

Fawn (verb)

While Ann's <u>fawning</u> endeared her to her superiors, it caused her co-workers to generally abominate her.

> *Other Common Forms: fawning (adjective, noun)*

Obsequious (adjective)

Darren's <u>obsequious</u> manner compelled him not just to avoid negative comments but to also always give exaggerated compliments.

> *Other Common Forms: obsequiousness (noun)*

Sycophant (noun ⚥)

The leader's reign crumbled after too many years of listening to <u>sycophants</u>, who agreed with her no matter how terrible the idea.

> *Other Common Forms: sycophantism (noun)*

TO INSULT

Affront (verb, noun)

In some cultures looking someone in the eye is not considered polite but a serious <u>affront</u> that shows disrespect.

Calumny (noun)

Political campaigns are too often marked by <u>calumny,</u> a false or misleading portrayal of a person's character or positions.

Other Common Forms: calumnious (adjective)

Contumely (noun)

The DJ's gift was not constructive criticism but <u>contumely,</u> which he aimed far and wide with the intention of offending his targets.

Other Common Forms: contumacious (adjective)

Denigrate (verb)

Elizabeth accentuated that her comments were not meant to <u>denigrate</u> the student but rather to help improve the student's work.

Other Common Forms: denigration (noun)

SMART

Acute (adjective)

The reporter was lauded by his peers for his <u>acute</u> and insightful depiction of the lives of migrant farm workers.

Other Common Forms: acuteness (noun)

Astute (adjective)

Elisha's friends took her grocery shopping with them because she always made <u>astute</u> choices of fruit.

Other Common Forms: astuteness (noun)

Canny (adjective)

The lawyer gained a reputation for being <u>canny,</u> a quality that allowed him make outrageous points to the juries without drawing the anger of the judges.

Other Common Forms: canniness (noun)

Erudite (adjective)

John Adams is often celebrated as an example of an <u>erudite</u> president whose knowledge was not only broad but deep.

Other Common Forms: erudition (noun)

RAPID REVIEW #11

Find the synonym.

1) Aversion

    (A) acuteness

    (B) calumny

    (C) abomination

    (D) excoriation

2) Lambaste

    (A) reprove

    (B) loathe

    (C) fawn

    (D) affront

3) Erudite

    (A) calumnious

    (B) obsequious

    (C) astute

    (D) contumacious

4) Affront

    (A) berate

    (B) upbraid

    (C) denigrate

    (D) excoriate

5) Sycophantism

    (A) astuteness

    (B) fawning

    (C) contumely

    (D) excoriation

6) Contumely

    (A) denigration

    (B) erudition

    (C) abomination

    (D) antipathy

7) Fawning

    (A) contumely

    (B) obsequiousness

    (C) canniness

    (D) aversion

8) Upbraid

    (A) berate

    (B) abominate

    (C) denigrate

    (D) fawn

STUPID

Dunce (noun ⚓)

Ironically the word "<u>dunce</u>" is taken from John Duns Scotus, one of the most intelligent and influential philosophers in Europe during the Middle Ages.

Fatuous (adjective)

The statement now lives on not so much because it was ignorant but because it was <u>fatuous,</u> blending arrogance and stupidity in a perfect proportion.

Foolhardy (adjective)

Franklin Coffin's attempt to scale Mt. Everest in a canoe was derided as <u>foolhardy</u> by even his most avid supporters.

Other Common Forms: inanity (noun)

Inane (adjective)

Isabelle's friends urged her not to waste her time on the <u>inane</u> movie, which made no sense at all.

Other Common Forms: inanity (noun)

BRAVE

Audacious (adjective)

While his wife called it imbecilic, Jeff preferred to think of his bet on the Super Bowl, for which he used their life savings, as <u>audacious</u>.

Other Common Forms: audacity (noun)

Intrepid (adjective)

Only the most <u>intrepid</u> parents volunteered to clean the boys' locker room after football practice in August.

Other Common Forms: intrepidness (noun)

Stalwart (adjective)

Having planted the first American flag at the North Pole, Matthew Henson was a <u>stalwart</u> explorer who received proper recognition only 30 years after his most daring feats.

Stout (adjective)

Rachel earned a reputation as a <u>stout</u> activist who would not stop fighting for her beliefs no matter the danger that might come.

Other Common Forms: stoutness (noun)

DIFFERENT / ODD

Aberrant (adjective)

The appearance of polar bears on the island was an <u>aberration</u>; normally they live more than 6,000 miles to the north.

Other Common Forms: aberration (noun)

Anomalous (adjective)

The <u>anomalous</u> nature of the newly-discovered species made it difficult for scientists to classify it.

Other Common Forms: anomaly (noun)

Quixotic (adjective)

While some argue that the quest for world peace is <u>quixotic</u> and useless because it can never be achieved, others believe that the idea itself is a useful antidote to complacent acceptance

WIDESPREAD / OBVIOUS

Egregious (adjective)

During the presentation, Ramon made a mistake so <u>egregious</u> that he feared that he was going to fail.

Manifest (adjective)

Shelly's fervidness for sports only becomes <u>manifest</u> after you truly get to know her.

Pervasive (adjective)

Once affordable to only the wealthy and thus limited, cell phones are now one of the most <u>pervasive</u> goods in the world.

Other Common Forms: pervasiveness (noun)

SECRET / HARD TO UNDERSTAND

Arcane (adjective)

The formula was so <u>arcane</u> that Todd could not grasp it no matter how many times he read it.

Clandestine (adjective)

Spies must remain <u>clandestine</u> in order to succeed, cloaking their every action and intention in total secrecy.

Inscrutable (adjective)

Tara's face was <u>inscrutable</u> as she watched the movie, making it impossible for her boyfriend to tell whether she was enjoying it.

Surreptitious (adjective)

The agreement to keep the negotiations <u>surreptitious</u> was unsuccessful, as even its most minute details found their way into the press.

LEVEL C REVIEW

Find the synonym.

1) Aberrant

   (A) intrepid

   (B) anomalous

   (C) avid

   (D) vexed

2) Debunk

   (A) upbraid

   (B) tout

   (C) iterate

   (D) refute

3) Clandestine

   (A) stout

   (B) inscrutable

   (C) manifest

   (D) incredulous

4) Stalwart

   (A) confounded

   (B) listless

   (C) fawning

   (D) intrepid

5) Fatuous

  (A) pervasive

  (B) foolhardy

  (C) equivocal

  (D) dumbfounded

6) Affront

  (A) contumely

  (B) berate

  (C) panegyrize

  (D) punctuate

7) Egregious

  (A) acute

  (B) manifest

  (C) contumacious

  (D) lackadaisical

8) Inane

  (A) audacious

  (B) arcane

  (C) fatuous

  (D) fervid

9) Canny

   (A) derisive

   (B) incredulous

   (C) obsequious

   (D) astute

10) Audacious

   (A) aberrant

   (B) calumnious

   (C) stout

   (D) languid

11) Surreptitious

   (A) fawning

   (B) avid

   (C) clandestine

   (D) aberrant

12) Demystify

   (A) excoriate

   (B) advocate

   (C) explicate

   (D) berate

13) Sycophantism

    (A) intrepidness

    (B) affront

    (C) fawning

    (D) vindication

14) Antipathy

    (A) calumny

    (B) anomaly

    (C) aversion

    (D) kudos

15) Stout

    (A) stalwart

    (B) inane

    (C) canny

    (D) incredulous

16) Quixotic

    (A) clandestine

    (B) anomalous

    (C) derisive

    (D) confounded

17) Advocate

   (A) excoriate

   (B) substantiate

   (C) rebut

   (D) delineate

18) Panegyric

   (A) audacity

   (B) approbation

   (C) antipathy

   (D) explication

19) Iterate

   (A) upbraid

   (B) scoff

   (C) invalidate

   (D) highlight

20) Rebuff

   (A) debunk

   (B) pervasiveness

   (C) foolhardiness

   (D) lampoon

Answer Keys

Rapid Review 1

1) C
2) D
3) B
4) A
5) D
6) B
7) D
8) A

Rapid Review 2

1) D
2) B
3) C
4) B
5) D
6) A
7) D
8) B

Rapid Review 3

1) C
2) B
3) A
4) D
5) B
6) D
7) B
8) D

Level A Review

1) C
2) D
3) A
4) B
5) D
6) C
7) B
8) C
9) D
10) A
11) A
12) D
13) D
14) B
15) D
16) C
17) D
18) D
19) B
20) C

Rapid Review 5

1) C
2) B
3) C
4) C
5) C
6) B
7) A
8) B

Rapid Review 6

1) D
2) B
3) A
4) C
5) D
6) A
7) C
8) B

Rapid Review 7

1) B
2) D
3) C
4) A
5) B
6) C
7) B
8) B

Level B Review

1) C
2) B
3) C
4) C
5) C
6) A
7) C
8) B
9) C
10) D
11) B
12) C
13) C
14) D
15) B

16) C
17) D
18) B
19) B
20) C

Rapid Review 9

1) B
2) B
3) D
4) B
5) C
6) B
7) A
8) C

Rapid Review 10

1) C
2) B
3) D
4) C
5) B
6) B
7) D
8) C

Rapid Review 11

1) C
2) A
3) C
4) C
5) B
6) A
7) B
8) A

<u>Level C Review</u>

1) B
2) D
3) B
4) D
5) B
6) A
7) B
8) C
9) D
10) C
11) C
12) C
13) C
14) C
15) A
16) B
17) B
18) B
19) D
20) A

QUICK LISTS

To Explain

account for   depict   illustrate   point out   portray

clarify   elucidate   illuminate   profile

delineate   demystify   explicate

To Argue For

confirm   defend   support

assert   bolster   contend   justify

advocate   corroborate   substantiate   vindicate

To Argue Against

contradict   counter   defy   discredit   disprove

dismiss   dispel   dispute

debunk   invalidate   rebuff   rebut   refute

To Emphasize

reinforce   stress

accentuate   reiterate   underscore

highlight   iterate   punctuate

Confused

baffled	perplexed	puzzled
befuddled	nonplussed	quizzical
confounded	dumbfounded	vexed

Mocking

ironic	parody	satirical
jeering	scornful	spoof
derisive	lampoon	scoff (at)

Doubtful / Questioning

critical	hesitant	skeptical
cynical	dubious	
dubitable	equivocal	incredulous

Indifferent / Lazy

dispirited	dispassionate	uninterested	
apathetic	jaded	lukewarm	nonchalant
lackadaisical	languid	listless	

Passionate

amorous	longing	yearning	
ardent	zeal	zest	
avid	élan	fervidness	fervor

Praise

acclaim	accolade	applause	hail	laud
commendation	eulogy	exalt		extol
approbation	kudos	panegyrize	plaudit	tout

Criticize / Scold

admonish	chastise	rebuke	reprimand
castigate	censure	decry	reproach
berate	excoriate	lambaste	reprove	upbraid

Dislike / Hate

animosity	antagonism	disinclination	
abhor	deplore	detest	rancor
abominate	antipathy	aversion	loathe

Flatter

adulate	bootlick	servile	
cajole	coax	lackey	toady
fawn	obsequious	sycophant	

Insult

scorn	slight	spite	taunt
defame	derision	disparage	malign
affront	calumny	contumely	denigrate

Smart

cunning	genius	shrewd	wise
ingenious	sagacious	sage	
acute	astute	canny	erudite

Stupid

buffoon	dolt	imbecilic	obtuse
dullard	dupe	vacuous	
dunce	fatuous	foolhardy	inane

Brave

bold	gallant	resolute
dauntless	undaunted	valiant
audacious	intrepid	stalwart	stout

Different / Odd

abnormal	deviant	variant
discrepancy	disparate	heterogeneous
aberrant	anomalous	quixotic

Widespread / Obvious

blatant	evident	explicit
conspicuous	flagrant	overt
egregious	manifest	pervasive

Secret / Difficult to Understand

covert	cryptic	stealthy
esoteric	furtive	incognito
arcane	clandestine	inscrutable	surreptitious

TEST PROFESSORS TITLES

5 SAT Math Practice Tests

5 SAT Reading Practice Tests

5 SAT Writing Practice Tests

10 SAT Vocabulary Practice Tests

FORTHCOMING TITLES

5 PSAT Math Practice Tests

5 PSAT Writing Practice Tests

10 PSAT Vocabulary Practice Tests

Score-Raising Vocabulary Builder for the GRE & GMAT

CPSIA information can be obtained at www.ICGtesting.com
Printed in the USA
LVOW05s0020231213

366496LV00009B/174/P